BECOMING A
PASTORAL
PARISH COUNCIL

How to make your PPC really useful
for the Twenty-First Century

PATRICIA CARROLL
Foreword by Archbishop Dermot Farrell

Published by Messenger Publications, 2022

ISBN 9781788125208

Designed by Messenger Publications Design Department
Cover Image © Petr Smagin / Shutterstock
Typeset in Times New Roman & Bembo
Printed by GPS Colour Graphics

Messenger Publications,
37 Leeson Place, Dublin D02 E5V0
www.messenger.ie

Contents

Acknowledgements

I wish to thank my colleagues in the former Office of Evangelisation and Ecumenism who have for many years provided training for Parish Pastoral Councils in the Archdiocese of Dublin. They prepared the ground for the future strengthening of the PPCs in Dublin. In particular I would like to thank Rosemary Lavelle who was a pastoral coordinator. It was always a great learning experience to work alongside her. I am also very grateful to Peter Siney, a parish pastoral worker who came up with the genius idea of three Ps of PPC, which I have been able to build upon. Finally, I would like to thank Archbishop Dermot Farrell who constantly affirms the model of co-responsible leadership in his own ministry in the Archdiocese.

FOREWORD

In *Becoming a Pastoral Parish Council*, Patricia Carroll outlines a very practical approach for parishes to set up and run Parish Pastoral Councils, which are an essential way to walk together building an effective, collaborative synodal church in a parish. Considering Pope Francis's efforts to renew the Church, this is a timely publication with regard to a body of ecclesial co-responsibility in parish pastoral care. The parish of today – and of tomorrow – needs a sharing of responsibility rather than a carving up of power. Otherwise, nothing will change; there will be no development, no growth. In the past, the parish was a community in which the priest(s) had a monopoly on everything and decided everything on their own. This situation can be overcome by the establishment of a properly functioning Parish Pastoral Council that is a participatory body: 'the body is one and has many members, and all the members of the body, though many, are one body … And God has so arranged the body … that there may be no dissension within the body, but the members may have the same care for one another', as St Paul so powerfully put it to the Corinthians (1 Cor 12:12, 24–25). Such a body allows parishioners to play a part in the pastoral development of their parish.

The author makes clear that the role of the Parish Pastoral Council is to identify pastoral needs and to help plan and coordinate pastoral programmes and services, working in close collaboration with the priests of the parish who are *ex officio* members of the council. The Parish Pastoral Council is a leadership structure that enables priests and people to work together to build up a dynamic Christian community that is characterised by prayer, hospitality, mission and evangelisation. The members of the council – which ought to be a microcosm of the parish – seek to bring their knowledge and experience of life in the parish to bear on this task.

In establishing a PPC the local church is contributing to the vision laid out by Pope Francis in *Evangelii Gaudium* where he has dwelt at length on the 'pastoral conversion' of the parish. The work of renewal in the Church is never complete. In *Evangelii Gaudium*, quoting the Second Vatican Council, he wrote, '"Every renewal of the Church essentially consists in an increase of fidelity to her own calling […] Christ summons the Church as she goes her pilgrim way… to that continual reformation of which she always has need, in so far as she is a human institution here on earth" (*Unitatis Redintegratio*, 6). […] I dream of a 'missionary option,' that is, a missionary impulse capable of transforming everything, so that the Church's customs, ways of doing things, times and schedules, language and structures can be suitably channelled for the evangelisation of today's world rather than for her self-preservation. […] The parish is not an outdated institution; precisely because it possesses great flexibility; it can assume quite different contours depending on the openness and missionary creativity of the pastor and the community' (*Evangelii Gaudium*, 26–28).

This time of reduced numbers of clergy may well afford us an opportunity to be creative and to re-imagine the institutions of the Church. The Lord is faithful (2 Thess 3:3). We have not been abandoned by our God; God's will can be found in the situation we find ourselves in right now with reduced numbers of clergy. Rather than looking back with de-energising nostalgia to the Church of our youth, let us look ahead to the Church in which we will minister and worship. In the end, the gospels, rooted as they are in the story of Jesus of Nazareth, are even more the story of the Risen Lord among his disciples. They root us in our beginnings, but more importantly provide a vision of the road Christ calls us to take.

The more fruitful question is what kind of Church God is calling us to be. The issue facing the Church today is not merely the more limited, although more urgent issue of coping with declining numbers of ordained minsters. God calls us and God calls us in a way that makes the most of the gifts (charisms) he has given us. Both dimensions involve discernment – we have to 'hear' and heed God's call, and we have to discern our true gifts. Neither task is 'easy' but each one leads to joy and peace, as was witnessed to by Pope St John XXIII in his appropriation of *voluntas tua pax nostra* – the saying of St Gregory Nazianzen he made his own. For Pope Francis it is the Gospel that 'tells us constantly to run the risk of a face-to-face encounter with others, with their physical presence which challenges us, with their pain and their pleas, with their joy which infects us in our close and continuous interaction' (*Evangelii Gaudium*, 82). Perhaps what we ultimately need to bring about the kind of renewal Pope Francis seeks is to be a community of disciples who would undertake and share responsibility for the life and ministry of the Church.

+ Dermot Farrell
Archbishop of Dublin

INTRODUCTION

This book has been written in a year when Parish Pastoral Councils (PPC) could not meet physically due to the Covid-19 pandemic. For many PPCs this meant that some stopped meeting, met on Zoom, or at least re-grouped to form the backbone of the parish sanitising committee.

PPCs are a relatively new structure in the Roman Catholic Church and are a fruit of the great Second Vatican Council. Following the principle of synodality, the PPC is a pastoral forum where lay people work side by side with the ordained to foster and develop the local mission of the Church. In this forum the dignity and equality of all the baptised are affirmed, valued and strengthened.[1] This dignity and equality was highlighted in the teaching of the Second Vatican Council about baptism, where it stated that all of the baptised share in the priestly, prophetic and kingly role of Christ by offering their lives in worship, speaking out against injustice and reaching out in loving service to others.[2] Within the pastoral forum of the PPC, lay and ordained work together to focus on the whole mission of the parish, enabling every baptised person in the parish to place their gifts at the service of the local community. This working together is called 'co-responsible leadership', meaning that lay people take their rightful place alongside the ordained to empower the whole parish for service.

It is hoped that those who read this book will have an 'aha' moment, where they find that the purpose of the PPC becomes more clear to them, and that they can begin to imagine the part they can play in the pastoral development of their parish.

---

1   *Code of Canon Law*, Vatican: The Holy See, 1983, 208.
2   Pope Paul VI, *Apostolicam Actuositatem*, Vatican: The Holy See, 18 November 1965, 10.

Chapter one begins by gently exploring the role of the PPC and relating this to the purpose of the parish community, debunking the myth that the PPC is a committee. Chapter two then looks at what can be called the five Ps of the PPC: Pastoral, Prayerful, Partnership, Planning and Participation.

In chapter three the whole notion of discernment for pastoral action is explored, especially with regard to how this relates to the ongoing, prayer-filled reflection of the PPC and the parish community.

Chapter four looks more deeply into the whole notion of partnership and its implications for how the PPC relates to the parish community.

Chapter five goes on to explore what makes planning in the PPC pastoral, and how that can be developed as a way of working in all parish groups.

Chapter six explores mission statements and how these can provide a platform for parish renewal and reflection, connecting them to parish assembly and listening together.

Every chapter begins with a short scripture reflection that acts as a springboard into the theme. At the end of every chapter there are also some reflection questions. These first focus on you, the reader, and try to help you to reflect on what you have read. There are also questions which are for your whole PPC that could be the basis for reflecting together as a group.

Chapter One

Chapter One

THE PARISH AND THE ROLE OF THE PPC

Awe came upon everyone, because many wonders and signs
were being done by the apostles.
All who believed were together and had all things in common;
they would sell their possessions and goods
and distribute the proceeds to all, as any had need.
Day by day, as they spent much time together in the temple,
they broke bread at home and ate their food with glad and generous
*   hearts,*
praising God and having the goodwill of all the people.
And day by day the Lord added to their number those who were
*   being saved.*

ACTS 2:4–47

This opening piece of scripture paints a picture of what life was like for the first Christians. The key features of this life were built around the pillars of prayer together, sharing of goods and reaching out to those who were needy. There was as yet no parish system as we know it, but there was a coming together for worship, a gathering of God's people, a generosity towards others and a care for others, which would later become a key feature of what became the parish system. What the Acts of the Apostles highlights is that from the beginning the Church was the gathering of God's people, a people who gathered to pray, to serve and to reach out. The early Christians who first gathered in one another's houses were small in number, as numbers grew they moved into larger spaces for worship, but still in the grounds of someone's home. When Christianity became the official religion of Rome and numbers dramatically increased, the basilicas used for the law courts became the gathering places in towns and cities. It is around this time of expansion that the Latin term *paroecia* or Greek term *parochia* begins to be used, this term connects with the idea of being near or beside a house. Specifically, the parish was the place where the people came from their homes, a gathering in God's house of those who lived nearby, encompassing a neighbourhood or local community. We can still recognise this description today in what we know as modern parish life.

WHAT IS A PARISH?

Many centuries later, evoking the homeliness and local roots of parish, Pope John Paul II described the parish as 'the Church living in the midst of the homes of her sons and daughters'.[3] Commenting on this Pope Francis has said that this 'idea presumes that it really is in contact with the homes and the lives of its people, and does not become a useless structure out of touch with people or a self-absorbed group made up of a chosen few.'[4] Here he is alluding to the notion of parochialism, where a parish becomes focused in on itself, forgets to look out beyond the gates towards those who are needy and neglected and loses sight of its primary purpose. Today this is often a key challenge for PPCs as many parishes are stuck in the rut of 'the way things have always been done'.[5] This might explain why Pope Francis is so strong about naming what the purpose of the parish is: for him, as well as a gathering of God's people in a local area, the parish is 'an environment for hearing God's word,

---

3   John Paul II, *Christifideles Laici*, Vatican: The Holy See, 30 September 1988, 26.
4   Pope Francis, *Evangelii Gaudium*, Vatican: The Holy See, 24 November 2013, 28.
5   This is a quote from a PPC chair who shared that this is often the biggest obstacle to any new development or outside-the-box thinking.

for growth in the Christian life, for dialogue, proclamation, charitable outreach, worship and celebration.'[6] Re-iterating the teaching of the Second Vatican Council, Francis once more emphasises the notion that the parish is a dynamic community of communities. It's a place where those who are thirsty for God can come and find a warm welcome, a centre where there is a constant reaching out to others. And he states that if we don't recognise this description, 'we must admit, though, that the call to review and renew our parishes has not yet sufficed to bring them nearer to people, to make them environments of living communion and participation, and to make them completely mission-oriented.'[7] This is the challenge for the twenty-first century parish, and it is in this context that the PPC can begin to understand its role and purpose.

Within the context of renewal, review and mission, the role of the PPC becomes clear. If the parish is a family of families, a community of communities led by the Holy Spirit, this implies that pastoral leadership is essential to its growth and development.

PASTORAL LEADERSHIP

It is the role of the PPC to take part in the pastoral leadership of the parish with the pastor or what we would call the parish priest. Without this shared leadership the parish cannot grow, develop or fully respond to what the Holy Spirit is saying in God's people. When there is good pastoral leadership in place, the parish becomes more confident in reaching out in service beyond the gates of the church. In this way the PPC reminds everyone in the parish of the call of baptism. Every baptised person is called to the ministry of building up. The building up is not about bricks and mortar. It's about building up people, to help them realise that God is with us, and to enable them to hear a call to service. This can only be done when the PPC opens itself to be led by the Holy Spirit, and when it seeks the guidance of the Holy Spirit in all it does in its time of service.

6   *Evangelii Gaudium,* 28.
7   *Evangelii Gaudium,* 28.

WHAT IS A PPC?

When reflecting about the role of the PPC it helps first to be clear about what a PPC is not: it does not concern itself with matters of finance or the day-to-day running of the parish. Although it might from time to time need to connect to the finance council[8] to clarify budgets for pastoral projects. It is not a group that manages the parish, the central parish team does that. It is a group that networks with the parish to help every parishioner take their part. Its function is not about helping Father, but about helping the parish to grow into a community where everyone finds a place and grows in some kind of service. Its primary concern is mission, that is helping everyone to realise their potential to serve. It has often been called the eyes and ears of the parish, not in a gossipy way, but that it's really in touch with what is going on in people's lives locally and how that impacts on living faith. It is a leadership group, who have responded to a call to service for a limited period of time. It imitates the Jesus way of leading, which is servant leadership. This servant leadership is epitomised in the image of the Last Supper where Jesus knelt down and washed the feet of his disciples, perhaps because of this the PPC can be referred to as the foot washers of the parish.

Fundamental to understanding the role of a PPC member is embracing the idea that every person in the parish is called to do something and to place their gifts at the service of one another. PPC members need to see themselves as enablers. PPC members who are enabling will be trying to identify, affirm and nourish the gifts that are in the whole parish community. PPC members need to constantly remember that at baptism every parishioner was called and gifted by God for a special purpose. PPC members need to view the parish as a community of the called and gifted. When the PPC meets, it needs to do so in the spirit of servant leadership: grounded in prayer and deep reflection about how God is calling each person and what God is calling the parish to be and do for the world.

8   *Code of Canon Law*, 537. This is described as a must in every parish, where there is a group of people in the parish who assist the pastor in the temporal affairs and financial administration of the parish.

THE COMMUNION MODEL

The bishops of Ireland affirmed this positive enabling vision of the PPC in their document *Living Communion*.[9] Here the PPC is described as:

'a faith-filled leadership group

through which priests and people work together

as co-responsible partners

in furthering the mission of Christ

in their own parish.'

This sentence unpacks this understanding, which is based on what we call the communion model of Church, that is that the Church or parish is a family of families. First, describing the PPC as a faith-filled leadership group avoids the idea that it is a committee. It is a gathering of Christ's faithful people, and faith must always be at the centre of all its activity. Second, it's a collaborative group, meaning that its modelling the way clergy and laity need to be together in action and purpose. Third, what flows from this is that it's a partnership, both lay and clergy are equally responsible together for the life of the parish. Fourth, connecting this with the mission of Christ helps us to focus on the bigger picture and the idea that our parish is actually a missionary community called to reach out beyond our comfort zones to those who are in need. Finally, the phrase 'in their own parish', roots this ministry locally, and helps to define the parameters of what the PPC is called to do. Everything the PPC does is focused on the local, but it will always have larger global connections to the movement of the Spirit in the world.

---

9   Bishops' Conference of Ireland, *Living Communion: Vision and Practice for Parish Pastoral Councils in Ireland Today*, Dublin: Veritas, 2011.

For Your Own Reflection

- What key words or phrases stand out for you in this chapter?
- What ideas are new for you or are you hearing for the first time?
- In what ways do you feel called to serve?
- What personal gifts of grace are you aware of and thankful for?

On Your Current PPC Practice

- What would your PPC need to change now, in view of what this chapter says?
- How has the Covid-19 pandemic changed your approach to the ministry of the PPC?
- What emerging needs are you noticing in the parish?

Useful Sources to Explore

- www.pastoralcouncils.com
- James A. Coriden, *The Parish in the Catholic Tradition, Mahwah*, NJ: Paulist Press, 1997.
- Donal Harrington, *Tomorrow's Parish: A Vision and a Path*, Dublin: Columba Books, 2018.
- Bishops' Conference of Ireland, *Living Communion: Vision and Practice for Parish Pastoral Councils in Ireland Today*, Dublin: Veritas, 2011.
- John Paul II, *Christifideles Laici*, Vatican: The Holy See, 30 September 1988.
- Pope Francis, *Evangelii Gaudium*, Vatican: The Holy See, 24 November 2013.

Chapter Two

Chapter Two

THE FIVE Ps OF THE PPC

Now there are varieties of gifts, but the same Spirit;
and there are varieties of services, but the same Lord;
and there are varieties of activities,
but it is the same God who activates all of them in everyone.
To each is given the manifestation of the Spirit for the common
  good.
To one is given through the Spirit the utterance of wisdom,
and to another the utterance of knowledge according to the same Spirit,
to another faith by the same Spirit, to another gifts of healing by
  the one Spirit,
to another the working of miracles, to another prophecy,
to another the discernment of spirits,
to another various kinds of tongues, to another the interpretation
  of tongues.
All these are activated by one and the same Spirit,
who allots to each one individually just as the Spirit chooses.

1 CORINTHIANS 12:4–11

This passage from the first letter to the Corinthians refers to the complementarity of gifts that Paul knew were needed in every Christian community for its continued growth and flourishing. Just as variety of giftedness was needed then so it is still needed today. Thankfully in every parish there are all sorts of people with all sorts of gifts. When we apply this to the PPC we can see why it is so important that lay and ordained work together, young and old work together, those who are more practical and those who are more visionary work together. We know that when every person is placing their gifts at the service of the parish great things can happen. Gone are the days when we lay people projected every spiritual gift onto Father and expected him to do everything.

PARTICIPATION

The passage from the first letter to the Corinthians links in with the first of the five Ps: participation. In the Church all are called to play their part. We were reminded of this at the Second Vatican Council where all were called to 'full, conscious and active participation'.[10] This principle of active participation doesn't just apply to the celebration of the liturgy. It is both a right and a duty of all the baptised to fully take part in the life of the Church, and this is what every PPC in the world is called to enable. Everything that the PPC does should be directed by this principle, to help everyone recognise their giftedness and to fully activate it at the service of the parish. Some people's gifts are more noticeable than others, for example a person who is musically gifted in a parish is a real asset, but there are others in the parish who have less noticeable gifts, like those who pray and intercede for those who are sick or have a quiet, reassuring presence. It's the role of the PPC to notice the giftedness of others and invite them to take their part, and as we have said before it is not any kind of participation but taking their part in the building up of the parish.

PASSIVITY

Encouraging participation in the life of the parish can be a difficult task especially if another P has taken hold of the imagination of parishioners, that is passivity. Symptoms of passive attitudes to parish life can be seen

10   Pope Paul VI, *Sacrosanctum Concilium*, Vatican: The Holy See, 4 December 1963, 14.

where parishioners hold back from what they call 'getting involved', or in phrases like, 'I'm just a lay person what do I know?' or in subtle attitudes of standing back. These passive mindsets could be a residue from pre-Second Vatican Council days when the liturgy was an activity that lay people stood back from and gazed at. It is not, however, a matter of age. It is more about a mindset, a feeling that 'this is not my place'. Another P in parish pastoral life that inhibits participation is procrastination: a habit in parish life of putting off what needs to be done. This habit often goes hand in hand with another pastoral habit: preserving the way things have always been done and calling that tradition. What might help a struggling PPC to break through to a new way of viewing things towards building up a healthy, positive culture of participation?

PASTORAL

Part of the answer to this lies in four other P words: pastoral, prayerful, partnership and planning. Let's look at the first of these and unpack the idea of pastoral. It's a word associated with taking care of sheep. The sheep here are the people of the parish. Just like good shepherds, the PPC are called to be a caring, listening presence, available to the people of the parish. The PPC is primarily focused on everything that relates to the faith life of the parish. This is from the beginning of life to the end of the road, often referred to as the journey of faith. The faith life of the parish involves encounters in prayer and service, helping the parish to see its role in reaching out in service to the local community. Individual PPC members have to keep in mind a holistic understanding of the parish. Individual PPC members don't promote the ideas of just one group, they take the whole picture on board when making pastoral decisions. PPC members lead by helping every parish member realise that they are called to serve and use their gifts for the sake of others. This leadership often means enabling others to see how they can make their contribution.

PLANNING

Leadership also means that planning takes place. Planning is about growing others in ministries and helping the parish embrace changes that help everyone grow. It is not just any kind of planning. It is pastoral, and so the focus is on planning for mission and planning with the parish. This planning enables the parish to truly activate the gifts of the Spirit received at baptism and strengthened at confirmation. This highlights that the ministry of the PPC is a practical one. It can help if a parish has a mission statement.[11] This enables the PPC and the parish to keep remembering what their core mission and purpose is. Initially significant time needs to be taken to formulate a mission Statement. The work of doing this together can help build unity and purpose in the parish. The mission statement should be revisited often. Any pastoral goals set must be connected to the mission statement and flow from it. These goals should also be grounded in actions that are achievable.

MOBILISING FOR MISSION

The role description of a PPC member is clear.[12] A PPC member is called to be discerning (discernment is a skill and a gift, see pages 28–31). The PPC member is a patient listener and does not always rush into action. The PPC member is called to awaken others to what living their baptism means and to form a spirituality of service that is rooted in responding to the baptismal call. PPC members are talent spotters. They are in touch with the giftedness of all and are the 'eyes and ears of the parish'. They mobilise others for mission. PPC members make decisions only after they have consulted a range of opinions and had considered conversations. They engage in dialogue, something different from discussion. They are willing to listen and learn. PPC

---

11 A mission statement gives clarity and purpose to broad goals. It can help the PPC to avoid being scattered in their efforts. It can inform a pastoral strategy that might be developed over a period of years. It helps the PPC to clarify vision, values and developments.

12 See *Living Communion*, 30–31

members review actions on a regular basis, and they do not do this alone. They do it with the parish and give everyone an opportunity to stop and reflect on how things are going and what might now be important. They do this through the parish assembly,[13] where all the qualities above come together and the whole parish begins to engage in this patient listening.

PARTNERSHIP

The PPC is also called to build partnerships, where mutual respect and cooperation are key. The partnership is about being partners in mission. Lay and ordained, young and old, experienced and less experienced, across the generations. Baptism is what grounds us in our ministries. All the baptised are called to place their gifts at the service of humankind. It might be a new message for some to hear that everyone is baptised into the priesthood of Christ, but what it means for us as a parish is that we were anointed to serve the world like Jesus, to worship God and to speak out against injustice. Partnership is strengthened when all realise that they share in the kingly, priestly and prophetic role of Jesus himself. The PPC may need to spend substantial time exploring the importance of baptism with the parish, in order to appreciate the distinctive call of the lay and the ordained.

PRAYER-FILLED CONSIDERATION

What underpins and strengthens partnership and planning is prayer-filled consideration. Prayer in the PPC is about much more than saying a prayer at the beginning and end of the formal meeting; it is about taking serious time to consider how God is calling. Simply put, it will be impossible to work together if the Spirit isn't in the work. PPC prayer always keeps the whole parish before God, and opens up the PPC to what God might be saying to the parish at this time. What we action

13 See chapter six of this book for a sample format for a parish assembly.

in the PPC needs to be a response to God's call to become the People of God, a people called to build the kingdom, not our own kingdoms. This is why when the PPC gathers, it should bring the presence of the parish into the gathering, always keeping the whole community in mind. Prayer helps the PPC to remember that they are trying to respond to God's call and do God's work.

For Your Own Reflection

- What key words or phrases stand out for you in this chapter?
- Which of the five Ps do you find most helpful?
- Where do you see signs of passivity, procrastination and preservation in your approach to parish life?

On Your Current PPC Practice

- Which of the five Ps are most developed in the PPC's ministry?
- Where do you see the most pastoral need in the parish?
- How do you approach prayer in the PPC? What are you open to changing about this?

Useful Sources to Explore

- Pope Paul VI, *Sacrosanctum Concilium,* Vatican: The Holy See, 4 December 1963.
- Planning Ministry, 'Understanding Pastoral Councils', https://www.planningministry.com/pastoral-councils/.
- Leadership Roundtable, 'Sample Mission Statements for Catholic Parishes', http://theleadershiproundtable.org/churchepedia/docs/services-docs/parish-mission-statement.pdf.
- Phyllis Brady and Brian Grogan SJ, *Meetings Matter: Spirituality and Skills for Meetings*, Dublin: Veritas, 2009.

Chapter Three

Chapter Three

PRAYER-FILLED REFLECTION IN THE PPC

Do not be conformed to this world,
but be transformed by the renewing of your minds,
so that you may discern what is the will of God
what is good and acceptable and perfect.
For as in one body we have many members,
and not all the members have the same function,
so we, who are many, are one body in Christ,
and individually we are members one of another.
We have gifts that differ according to the grace given to us:
prophecy, in proportion to faith; ministry, in ministering;
the teacher, in teaching; the exhorter, in exhortation;
the giver, in generosity; the leader, in diligence;
the compassionate, in cheerfulness.

ROMANS 12:2–3, 4–8

Here in the letter to the Romans Paul refers to gifts of discernment. In his understanding those who are called Christian are gifted by the Spirit to know the mind of God. This gift of the Spirit enables Christians to make wise choices. The gift of discernment is given for the sake of building up the community; a discerning community values the gifts that each person has been given. In relation to the PPCs it is in exercising the gift of discernment that wise pastoral choices can be made for the flourishing of the whole parish community. The activity of the PPC is as such grounded in prayerful consideration of where the Spirit is moving. Prayer should then inform and guide all that the PPC does.

INFORMED AND GUIDED BY PRAYER

Let's look at why prayer should inform and guide all the PPC does. The PPC is not just any kind of leadership group; it is a leadership group of God's faithful people. Each member of the PPC is a person of faith. Just as faith informs all we do in our daily life, so too it informs the ministry of the PPC. Prayer not only informs the work, but it is its guiding principle. In common prayer we tune in to what the Holy Spirit is saying to the Church, relying on the guidance of the spirit in everything we do. There is a very old saying from monasticism, *ora et labora*[14] (pray and work). It is interesting that in this phrase prayer comes first. This needs to be a priority for all PPC members because the work emerges from the prayer or prayerfully considering what the Lord is calling us to do. Prayer grounds us and helps us to realise that all we do has to be grounded in God's project for the parish, not our projects generated by our own egos. There is a qualitative difference to the decision-making in the PPC when what is planned is given considered attention in reflection and prayer. In fact, everyone on the PPC needs to be on a journey of their own personal renewal because this is what will renew the parish in a lasting way. When the PPC becomes just another committee, then it loses its spirit and sense of purpose. When the PPC is grounded in prayerful reflection then there will be a difference in how and what is planned together for the common good of the parish.

COMMUNAL PRAYER

Many people feel awkward in a communal prayer setting, so praying together as a PPC will take time to get used to. Some have become

14 This phrase comes from the Rule of St Benedict. Benedict founded monastic communities all over Europe.

accustomed to saying their prayers but might be shy or unused to praying in a group. There can be a perception that Father should lead all prayer, after all is that not his job! This is a trap we can fall into in the PPC where we look to Father to begin and end the meeting with a prayer. The challenge of PPC prayer is that everyone takes a lead, that over time everyone becomes comfortable with leading prayer. Another thing that can be in people's minds, particularly if they are of a business-like mindset, is that prayer is wasting time, time that could be spent talking about getting things done. This is another trap that PPCs can often fall into. It is only when we take time to be still and listen for the voice of the Lord that we can begin to notice what He might be asking of us. Prayerful reflection together can then inform everything we do and give us new energy for service.

We know that there is a great variety of ways of praying and that prayer means all sorts of things to people. For some prayer means reciting the rosary and reflecting on passages of scripture with its background repetitive rhythm. For others it is linked to singing the psalms or listening to music. Some enjoy stillness and silence, while others enjoy being in touch with nature and the wonder of creation. When we come together as a PPC we can be aware of this, but we also have to keep in mind that our prayer at the PPC is not personal but community prayer together. Together we listen to God and we speak to God about our concerns and needs at a particular time. As we pray together, we learn to trust that the Holy Spirit is with us and among us, speaking to each person's heart.

TUNING IN TO GOD

PPC prayer should lead us to tune in to God, so that we can find out what God wants for us. This is called discernment. Discernment is like tuning in to a digital radio. Once you are tuned in to the station you can listen easily. Discernment helps to sift out what is good, better and best in our pastoral action. Discernment together is a skill we can learn over time. It involves first an openness to God's voice, a quiet listening so as to understand. What can help this are well-chosen scripture passages, a time of silence in our PPC prayer, an invitation to share, and noticing how we are feeling about particular suggestions. This is called paying attention to the movement of God. Since God speaks to us through our feelings, we must pay attention to how we feel about particular situations and needs that arise in the parish.

Pope Francis has often referred to this gift of discernment in his writings, for him discernment 'calls for something more than intelligence or common sense. It is a gift which we must implore.'[15] For Francis 'the gift of discernment has become all the more necessary today, since contemporary life offers immense possibilities for action and distraction, and the world presents all of them as valid and good. All of us, but especially the young, are immersed in a culture of zapping. We can navigate simultaneously on two or more screens and interact at the same time with two or three virtual scenarios. Without the wisdom of discernment, we can easily become prey to every passing trend.'[16] This applies equally to parish pastoral life, particularly when all sorts of exciting possibilities are on the agenda for the PPC to consider. Without the gift of discernment, and a commitment by PPC to take time to discern choices, the meeting can become like an ideas factory that is never grounded in how the Holy Spirit might be leading and calling. When discernment is exercised PPC plans can then be more grounded in recognising 'the concrete means that the Lord provides in his mysterious and loving plan, to make us move beyond mere good intentions.'[17]

LEADING PRAYER

Everyone in the PPC should learn to lead prayer. Here are some guidelines for getting started. It is highly recommended that the prayer

15 Pope Francis, *Gaudete et Exsultate*, Vatican: The Holy See, 19 March 2018, 166.
16 *Gaudete et Exsultate*, 167.
17 *Gaudete et Exsultate*, 169.

is prepared beforehand in a partnership of two. This way you can help each other keep the focus and plan together. This is modelling a way of doing things in the parish, where we always work together and never alone.

This is a simple format for prayer. It is important to set up a separate space for the PPC prayer. Prayer works best when we are not gathered around a table like a business meeting. It is good practice to arrange a focal point or sacred space that the PPC can gather around. This is a good way to leave the day behind and enter into a new moment. This kind of prayer gives new energy, and helps the PPC to give their attention more fully to one another and to the Lord. It is more helpful if the meeting table is in a separate space from the prayer space and that the PPC move to the table when prayer is over.

SAMPLE PPC PRAYER TIME

Here is a sample of how prayer can be organised. It's a very simple process and it is not lengthy:

- Create a prayer space and gather around it in a circle in a separate space from the business table.
- Light a candle and remember God is present in a few moments of silence together.
- One person reads a short piece of scripture aloud. **All listen**.
- The scripture is read aloud a second time by a different person. **All listen**.
- After some time the group is invited to share a word or phrase that strikes them. **All listen**.
- The leaders then invite a time of intercession – praying for the needs.
- Each person is invited to say a prayer aloud or in the silence of their hearts as the candle is passed around.
- When the candle has been passed round to all, end by saying the Glory Be to the Father together.

You can also get into the habit of exploring suggested prayer resources, which can give you inspiration if you are planning together.[18]

The PPC is always mindful of God's call. God is calling us at all times. When we surround our activity with prayer we become more conscious of this. Over time the PPC as a group can become more sensitive to what God may be asking, helping to clarify how and where parish priorities should be set.

---

18 For daily reflections and online prayer exercises see: Sacred Space, www.sacredspace.ie. For daily reflections with music and scripture for the day, see: Pray as You God, https://pray-as-you-go.org/. For prayer experiences based on the Sunday readings, see: PREGO, https://stbeunosoutreach.wordpress.com/prego/.

For Your Own Reflection

- What is your preferred way of praying?
- How comfortable are you with praying in a group?
- How do you feel about being asked to lead prayer?

On Your Current PPC Practice

- How does prayer happen in your PPC at present?
- What would you like to change about it and why?
- How can your PPC become more discerning about decision-making?

Useful Sources to Explore

- Pope Francis, *Gaudete et Exsultate*, Vatican: The Holy See, 19 March 2018.
- Pope Francis, *Christus Vivit*, Vatican: The Holy See, 25 March 2019. Francis (vatican.va), Chapter nine focuses on discernment.
- Sr Mary Leanne Hubbard, www.godseekersnd.com, introduction-to-communal-discernment.pdf.
- Jane Ferguson, A *Handbook for Parish Pastoral Councils: Skills to Perform the Task*, Dublin: Columba Press, 2005.

Chapter Four

Chapter Four

DEVELOPING PARTNERSHIP

I thank my God every time I remember you.
In all my prayers for all of you,
I always pray with joy
because of your partnership in the Gospel
from the first day until now,
being confident of this,
that he who began a good work in you
will carry it on to completion
until the day of Christ Jesus.

PHILIPPIANS 1:3–6

MISSION

In this short excerpt from the letter to the Philippians Paul gives thanks for those who he refers to as his co-workers in spreading the Good News. One of these was a young follower of the Jesus Way called Timothy. In fact, Paul would not have had the impact that he did if he had not collaborated with others and saw them as partners with him in spreading the Good News. This letter was probably written while Paul was in prison, but he has enormous confidence that the mission began will continue to flourish through partnership with others. When we hear the word 'mission' we often think about travelling to a faraway place where people do not know about Jesus. In Ireland there was a strong tradition of going out to the whole world and spreading the Good News. But mission is more subtle than that. Pope Francis has reminded us that mission flows from our baptism. He says:

> In virtue of their baptism, all the members of the People of God have become missionary disciples (cf. Mt 28:19). All the baptised, whatever their position in the Church or their level of instruction in the faith, are agents of evangelisation, and it would be insufficient to envisage a plan of evangelisation to be carried out by professionals while the rest of the faithful would simply be passive recipients. The new evangelisation calls for personal involvement on the part of each of the baptised. Every Christian is challenged, here and now, to be actively engaged in evangelisation; indeed, anyone who has truly experienced God's saving love does not need much time or lengthy training to go out and proclaim that love. Every Christian is a missionary to the extent that he or she has encountered the love of God in Christ Jesus: we no longer say that we are 'disciples' and 'missionaries', but rather that we are always 'missionary disciples'.[19]

PARTNERS IN MISSION

When we think about the PPC we also need to connect it with this notion of mission. Each person on the PPC is a missionary disciple because of their baptism, and that's why together we are partners in mission. This is an important phrase and concept for every member of the PPC to grasp. Every baptised person is gifted and called to further Christ's mission. This is a new mindset that many parishioners will need help to embrace. In the PPC we do this best when we work as a partnership, lay and ordained together, male and female together, young and old together. By the way the PPC interacts it can model that we are all partners in the one mission of Jesus. For many in the parish the notion of partnership is new. To move from an attitude of 'Father's in charge' to one of working

19 *Evangelii Gaudium,* 120.

together for mission requires a mindset shift in everyone. This shift in mindset needs to be seen in the way that the PPC members relate to one another and to the parish. The language of partnership needs to be at the forefront of all parish communication. PPCs need to be intentional about growing new practices and approaches but also reflect together regularly about how this is developing.

ENABLING PARTNERSHIP TO GROW

What might help to develop this way of being parish together? PPC members are called to help all parishioners find their place. We grow slowly into a new way of being parish when we make partnership a priority. PPC members need to model what partnership looks like in their relating and acting. Partnership is both a mindset and a chosen practice. The PPC models partnership for the parish when it intentionally chooses to work in pairs or teams. Regularly checking out decisions and actions with each other in the PPC models partnership. When the PPC commits itself to grow team ministries, to pray and reflect together regularly and to build community, working in partnership becomes the way we do things around here. When we gather for the PPC meeting it is always helpful to check out how we are working together as a PPC. We can ask the following questions: Who are we working with? For instance, who is connecting with the funeral team, the children's liturgy group or the parish visitors group? How are parish groups growing in working together? Where is there evidence of lay and ordained working together? What needs to be strengthened or developed?

SIGNS OF GROWTH

Here are three indicators that your PPC can use to help you recognise how you need to develop the mindset and practices that will help partnership to grow:
- Collaboration is practised
- Team ministries are in place
- Community life is valued

When collaboration is practised it can be seen in the following ways. The PPC listens to parishioners' concerns, communicates consistently, and engages members by challenging, inviting and welcoming their involvement in the community's life. The PPC actively works together for the good of the whole parish, closed groups are discouraged and parish groups are encouraged to work together well. The PPC regularly encourages new recruitment and new ideas. It also creates opportunities for many to take ownership of mission and ministries. The PPC helps to grow teams with responsibilities and accountability. Every parish group has a role description[20] and all parish groups have a named team leader. The PPC invites and encourages teams to take part in regular team meetings where roles are discussed, clarified and strengthened. The PPC provides formation opportunities to support and sustain the roles of parish groups. The PPC with team leaders invites new membership and recruits for ministries on at least an annual basis. The PPC encourages a variety of gatherings for fun, formation, prayer and support, helping the parish to build community life. Relationships of care are built and nurtured. The PPC encourages the parish community to reach out in care in particular moments: death, illness, family crisis, life's difficulties. The PPC develops healthy connections to local groups and other Churches. The PPC encourages a variety of ages and stages to take their place in the celebration of the liturgy.

---

20 Donald H. Kahn, *The Collaborative Leader: Listening to the Wisdom of God's People*, Notre Dame: Ave Maria Press, 1995.

For Your Own Reflection

- How would you describe you own preferred working style?
- Are you most comfortable working alone or with others?
- What skills from your life and work would be valuable for building up a parish partnership?

On Your Current PPC Practice

- How does the PPC support collaboration in the parish?
- What team ministries are in place and how are these supported?
- How are role descriptions reviewed?
- What patterns of recruitment for groups and teams are there in the parish?

Useful Sources to Explore

- Harrington, *Tomorrow's Parish* – particularly chapter eight, 'Who's who in the Parish'.
- David Robertson, *Collaborative Ministry: What It Is, How It Works, and Why*, Ossett: Parbar Publishing, 2007.
- Johnny Doherty, Oliver Crilly, and Frank Dolaghan, *Think Big, Act Small: Working at Collaborative Ministry through Parish Pastoral Councils*, Dublin: Veritas, 2005.

Chapter Five

Chapter Five

WHAT MAKES PLANNING PASTORAL?

*'For I know the plans
I have for you,'
declares the Lord,
'plans to prosper you
and not to harm you,
plans to give you hope
and a future.'*

JEREMIAH 29:11

As we begin to think about pastoral planning, we can take time to reflect on this very simple verse from the prophet Jeremiah. These words from the prophet are meant to be reassuring. The people of Israel had lost their way and felt confused about the direction of their lives. Jeremiah comes into the picture as a prophet of a new future. God's basic plan for every human being is that they should flourish and grow. God is always acting for our good, and this is why we have hope. We know that he is on our side. It's not so much that God has an individualised business plan for each person, but that his plan is that all humanity has a destiny that is God shaped. The future is bright and hopeful because he is in it.

What might God's plan be for parish pastoral life? Pope Francis gives us some insights to ponder that may help to answer that question. First, he speaks about having a dream for the Church where 'the Church's customs, ways of doing things, times and schedules, language and structures can be suitably channelled for the evangelisation of today's world rather than for her self-preservation.'[21] He calls this a missionary option that is capable of transforming everything. When this is applied to parish life then it begins to give a focus to any pastoral planning that the PPC may do. Second, Pope Francis encourages the whole Church 'to be bold and creative in this task of rethinking the goals, structures, style and methods of evangelisation in their respective communities.'[22] This implies that pastoral planning is more about helping the parish to spread the Good News and less about keeping the show on the road. We can add this insight to the basic definition of a PPC as a 'a faith-filled leadership group through which priests and people work together as co-responsible partners in furthering the mission of Christ in their own parish.'[23] This means that pastoral planning is a faith-filled activity which lay and ordained do together. It's also about furthering the mission of Jesus in a local way, for a specific community with specific needs.

WHAT DOES PASTORAL MEAN?

The word pastoral comes from shepherding. It's about looking after and care, and that is why it is now used in a variety of settings: church, healthcare and school. Pope Francis chose an image of shepherding for his pectoral cross. It reminds us all that the essential work of the Church is caring for people. It is about the many and varied ways care is offered to people with various needs. Pastoral life in every parish is very varied, but it's always about connecting with people. The pastoral life of the parish is not something that is invisible. We can see this pastoral life in the way people are cared for, the way we pray together and celebrate sacraments together. We can notice this quality of care in the many

21 *Evangelii Gaudium*, 27.
22 *Evangelii Gaudium*, 33.
23 *Living Communion*.

ways groups are formed in faith, the way in which we reach out to those who are struggling and finally in community gatherings.

PASTORAL PLANNING

Planning is always about the future, and at the same time it's always about people. When planning loses its focus on caring for people, it stops being pastoral. However, pastoral planning is not any kind of planning, it's Spirit-led planning. To do this well the PPC has to listen: listen to the voice of the Spirit in the people of God. This can be done in a variety of ways. It can happen informally in the way PPC members are noticing needs and connecting with groups. The second way of listening is more formal where there is an annual parish assembly, giving an opportunity to reflect on current needs. An annual parish assembly can be an experience of affirmation of what is good and a critique of what could be further developed or initiated. An annual parish assembly is a moment in the life of the parish where pastoral priorities start to be named for the year ahead, and the PPC becomes more aware of how the life of the parish is growing or declining. It's often very helpful to bring in an external facilitator to guide this, and it might also be helpful for the whole PPC to do some basic training in listening skills.[24]

STEPS AND STAGES

After listening to the People of God in the parish the PPC needs to focus on naming steps and stages towards pastorally addressing the issues. There are usually three steps in effective pastoral planning. Having listened the PPC prayerfully considers where priorities should be focused. This planning takes on the scope of the whole pastoral year. Many PPCs get stuck at this stage and do not progress. Plans need to be developed. It's no use making a plan if it doesn't progress. Therefore, the second stage of pastoral planning is the development stage. In this stage the steps and stages toward reaching the goals determined in the

24 Chapter six of this book has more information on parish assemblies.

first stage are clearly identified. Finally, when the PPC has done this in a clear way, it can move to the third stage: implementation. This involves drawing others into the work by forming working groups that move things forward. This is what should form the agenda of PPC meetings. Smart planning is used in business. It's a good tool for parish pastoral planning too. It helps everyone to be more specific about what needs to be achieved. The pastoral goals that the PPC set themselves should be specific, easy to evaluate, easy to achieve and complete, be relevant to parishioners and be timed for progress. The diagram below illustrates this approach:

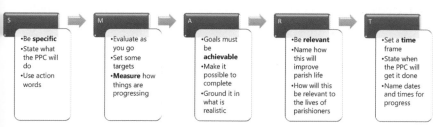

S
•Be **specific**
•State what the PPC will do
•Use action words

M
•Evaluate as you go
•Set some targets
•**Measure** how things are progressing

A
•Goals must be **achievable**
•Make it possible to complete
•Ground it in what is realistic

R
•Be **relevant**
•Name how this will improve parish life
•How will this be relevant to the lives of parishioners

T
•Set a **time** frame
•State when the PPC will get it done
•Name dates and times for progress

COMMUNICATING WITH THE PARISH

Keeping in touch with the parish is essential. PPCs need to use every modern means to do this. If there is no one on the PPC with the skills to do this then a person in the parish with these skills can be co-opted on to subgroups. Every parish website should have a space for PPC updates. It's not good enough to just name who is on the PPC and leave the page dead. Updates to the parish after each meeting are essential. If your PPC is not up to speed with this, it could be prioritised in part of your pastoral plan. No parish today can live without connecting to the internet, as parishioners connect to this on a daily basis it's essential to get this right. The current pastoral plan for the parish should be readily available for all parishioners to access online. Any pastoral changes or developments need to be communicated as soon as possible to the people of the parish.

PPC AGENDA ITEMS

The PPC can easily get bogged down in the day-to-day stuff of parish life. This is not the role of the PPC. Others can attend to this. When the PPC focuses too much on the day to day the meeting becomes very dull and the focus on pastoral planning and mission is often lost. Less is often more. When there are only one or two items for the agenda then pastoral planning can become the focus. Time always needs to be given over to reflecting on where things are at. An agenda that is jampacked can feel overwhelming, and often when this happens items are not dealt with fully or progressed. It is the role of the three main office holders to formulate the agenda for each meeting.[25] Items to be considered would be sent out to all PPC members beforehand in a timely way by the PPC secretary, so that any documents can be read. It is unproductive to read through documentation while the meeting is taking place. The agenda set should presume that everyone has taken time to process what has been sent out for consideration and is ready to make a response.

FOCUS ON THE PASTORAL PLAN

When the focus of the agenda is more about building the parish up for a new future there is more positive energy. The agenda becomes focused in a prayerful, discerning way. There may only be one or two items to examine, but they will be explored in depth, progressed in a practical way and new actions named. At the PPC meeting reflection takes place about what are the good, better and best decisions to make, in order to progress the pastoral life of the parish. In a PPC meeting that is focused, attention is given to the parish pastoral plan and how the goals that have been set can be achieved. When this happens there will be reports from the various subgroups or working groups that were engaged in different development issues. When the PPC focuses more intently on the pastoral plan it becomes clear that the real work of the PPC is not the meeting itself, but what happens in between meetings

25   Main officeholders on the PPC are the president (usually the parish priest), the chair and the secretary.

46

where dialogue with group leaders takes place, work with subgroups takes place and ideas become practical initiatives.

ELEMENTS OF PASTORAL PLANNING

Pastoral planning leads to new pastoral action and activities. This is an important element to be grasped by every member of the PPC, as there can be a perception that any planning done in the parish is about maintaining groups and activities. Pastoral planning 'calls for attention to the bigger picture, openness to suitable processes and concern for the long run.'[26] Pope Francis has emphasised the importance of people building in any pastoral projects that are initiated.[27] Therefore a key element in understanding pastoral planning is that it is done with people, not for people. This also affirms the principle of widening participation, where all are called to find their place in the life and work of the parish community. Another element of pastoral planning is that any processes used should build unity and purpose in the parish and not division or conflict.[28] Decisions that are made in the absence of the wider parish community can often lead to conflict. This is why its essential to keep the parish informed of every step and stage of a process. The parish should know what the beginning, middle and end of a process looks like, and have the opportunity to give feedback that will inform further development. Another important element of pastoral planning is honouring Pope Francis' principle that 'realities are more important than ideas.'[29] For example, we can be very idealistic and enthusiastic about the idea that everyone is called to play their part, but if the reality is that the parish has an ageing population and an absence of enthusiastic newcomers then our pastoral possibilities must be grounded on this rather than any ideal of what should be. When developing a pastoral plan it's important to take in a broader horizon than just our parish. This calls

26 *Evangelii Gaudium*, 225.
27 *Evangelii Gaudium*, 224.
28 *Evangelii Gaudium*, 226–230.
29 *Evangelii Gaudium*, 231–233.

for both a local and global awareness of the movement of the Spirit in the Church and in the world, where the PPC can help each other and the parish to 'see the greater good that will benefit all.'[30]

Yet another element of pastoral planning is ownership; it cannot be said enough that the PPC is not about making decisions for the rest of the parish. If people in the parish have little or no sense of connection to the planning then they will have no interest in it, and ultimately not support development. Ownership happens when people can imagine a new future and the part they can play in it. An easy way to help this happen is to frequently remind the parish of what they said and how the PPC is now responding to this. The final element of pastoral planning is that it leads to people changing their behaviours. For some this is a difficult thing to do, especially if the mindset that the Church never changes has taken hold. Having a mission statement or a well worked-out pastoral plan will not be of any use if actions are not named, and these actions must always be grounded in prayer.

ATTITUDES WE BRING TO PASTORAL PLANNING

When Pope Francis wrote *Evangelii Gaudium,* he offered a reflection to those who were jaded in their pastoral work. What he says to them can also apply to PPCs and the work of pastoral planning. First Francis invites everyone in the Church to say their own yes to focusing on mission and outreach.[31] When each member of the PPC makes a commitment to mission-focused pastoral planning, great things can happen. Francis proposes some basic attitudes that the PPC can adopt and that can help build up a mission-focused parish community. The first attitude to adopt is what he calls pastoral realism. This will be reflected in the pastoral plan where there are reasonable goals to be achieved and everyone feels they are on board.[32] The second attitude is about practising patience so that pastoral processes can mature.[33] The PPC often needs to practise

30 *Evangelii Gaudium*, 235.
31 *Evangelii Gaudium*, 78–80.
32 *Evangelii Gaudium*, 82.
33 *Evangelii Gaudium*, 82.

patience with new developments so that they can slowly and steadily develop over a period of years. The third attitude is that the PPC keeps in mind that the journey itself may ultimately be more important than the road map.[34] Francis has encouraged every Christian to avoid what he calls a 'sterile pessimism'.[35] This attitude is important for the PPC, particularly when it seems nothing is developing and the parish feels stuck.

Pastoral planning brings about a renewal of community when it is done well. Pope Francis invites us to say a yes to the new relationships and networks that emerge from this. When pastoral planning works it brings about a new energy borne of encountering others.[36] So the final attitude I want to highlight in pastoral planning is that of risk taking. The PPC needs to launch out into the deep and take the risk of interaction and encounter with others, taking the lead from the Gospel. For Pope Francis it is the Gospel that 'tells us constantly to run the risk of a face-to-face encounter with others, with their physical presence which challenges us, with their pain and their pleas, with their joy which infects us in our close and continuous interaction.'[37]

34 *Evangelii Gaudium,* 82.
35 *Evangelii Gaudium,* 84.
36 *Evangelii Gaudium,* 87.
37 *Evangelii Gaudium,* 88.

For Your Own Reflection

- What is your preferred style of working?
- In what way/s do you value planning in your life?
- In what way/s do you avoid planning in your life?

On Your Current PPC Practice

- What are the PPCs current priorities in pastoral planning?
- In light of what has been said above how might the PPC need to change?
- What elements and attitudes of pastoral planning need to be developed?

Useful Sources to Explore

- William L. Pickett, *A Concise Guide to Pastoral Planning*, Notre Dame: Ave Maria Press, 2007.
- Mary Anne Gubish, Susan Jenny, Arlene McGannon, *Revisioning the Parish Pastoral Council: A Workbook*, Mahwah, NJ: Paulist Press, 2001.
- Harrington, *Tomorrow's Parish*, particularly section D.

Chapter Six

Chapter Six

MISSION and MISSION STATEMENTS

When he came to Nazareth, where he had been brought up,
he went to the synagogue on the sabbath day, as was his custom.
He stood up to read, and the scroll of the prophet Isaiah was given
to him.

He unrolled the scroll and found the place where it was written:

'The Spirit of the Lord is upon me,
because he has anointed me
to bring good news to the poor.
He has sent me to proclaim release to the captives
and recovery of sight to the blind,
to let the oppressed go free,
to proclaim the year of the Lord's favour.'

And he rolled up the scroll, gave it back to the attendant, and sat
down. The eyes of all in the synagogue were fixed on him.

LUKE 4:16–21

This passage from Luke's Gospel will be very familiar to you. It comes after the story about Jesus being baptised. Immediately Jesus began to preach about the Kingdom of God and the newness of his message was attracting followers. To inaugurate his mission he returned to his home place and shocked the gathering by proclaiming his mission statement. Those gathered in the synagogue on that day were shocked because Jesus was applying this scripture passage to himself. He was literally saying, 'I am the one who brings Good News.' This is Jesus' mission statement. It's Jesus' self-understanding of what God is calling him to be and do. Here Jesus names his identity as well as what he will do to address God's concerns and the hopes of God's people. His mission statement is not confused or muddled. It's purposeful and direct. It's exciting and challenging. It's naming directions and activities. There is an energy about Jesus mission statement that is about reaching out to others and bringing something to them. It's naming very clearly the core purpose of his life. It is stating very loudly that God's purpose is also Jesus' purpose.

THE MISSION OF JESUS and OUR MISSION

Of course, Jesus' purpose is supposed to be our purpose too. This is what Pope Francis has reminded us about in *Evangelii Gaudium* when he speaks about the mission entrusted to every baptised person: 'My mission of being in the heart of the people is not just a part of my life or a badge I can take off; it is not an "extra" or just another moment in life. Instead, it is something I cannot uproot from my being without destroying my very self. I am a mission on this earth; that is the reason why I am here in this world. We have to regard ourselves as sealed, even branded, by this mission of bringing light, blessing, enlivening, raising up, healing and freeing.'[38] Here Francis intentionally moves away from the mindset that most Christians still have about mission, that is that someone else does it on our behalf! Here it is very clear that all of the baptised are called to bring light, blessing, life and healing to others. As a personal mission

38 *Evangelii Gaudium*, 273.

statement for every baptised person it's not a bad start. For Francis personal mission is rooted in the universal call to holiness, finding 'its fullest meaning in Christ, and can only be understood through him.'[39] Imagine if every baptised person in your parish suddenly realised that this was their core calling. What would the parish look like?

MISSION MOVES OUT

Francis imagines what this looks like when he speaks of the Church as a community of missionary disciples.[40] Here he helps us to imagine what a community of missionary disciples looks like:

- It's a community of those who take the first step, who are involved and supportive, who bear fruit and rejoice.
- It's a community who knows that the Lord has taken the initiative, he has loved us first.[41]
- It's a community who can move forward, boldly take the initiative, go out to others, seek those who have fallen away, stand at the crossroads and welcome the outcast.
- Such a community has an endless desire to show mercy, the fruit of its own experience of the power of the Father's infinite mercy.
- Because of this it's a community that gets involved by word and deed in people's daily lives.
- It's a community that bridges distances, it is willing to abase itself if necessary, and it embraces human life, touching the suffering flesh of Christ in others.
- It's a community that is also supportive, standing by people at every step of the way, no matter how difficult or lengthy this may prove to be. It is familiar with patient expectation and apostolic endurance.
- Finally, it's a community that is filled with joy; it knows how to rejoice always. It celebrates every small victory, every step forward in the work of evangelisation.

39 *Gaudete et Exsultate,* 20
40 *Evangelii Gaudium,* 24
41 1 John 4:19.

- It's a community that celebrates its joy in the beauty in the liturgy, as part of its daily concern to spread goodness.
- This community evangelises and is itself evangelised through the beauty of the liturgy, which is both a celebration of the task of evangelisation and the source of renewed self-giving.

I imagine you are asking yourself, 'Where is the parish?' Here Francis is painting a picture. He is giving indicators of what a twenty-first century parish community can look like. Francis is describing a community that reaches out beyond itself in service, and this is the essence of mission – movement out beyond self. Here mission links with the life of God. As someone else put it, God in us gives Godself away. It's about 'God's reaching out so that all might share in God's life.'[42]

PARISH MISSION STATEMENTS

If a parish mission statement is not grounded in the mission of Jesus and the call of Jesus to missionary discipleship it will probably look like a mission statement for a supermarket! For example, Tesco's mission statement is 'Every little helps!'. As a statement of intent for a supermarket, it points to Tesco's mission to help the customer access goods in a timely helpful manner. However, if this was the mission statement of a parish we could ask the following questions:

- How would a person know this is a Church being described?
- What's this got to do with the mission of Jesus?
- What's it calling the parish to be and to do?

When we think about a mission statement for a parish we have to keep in mind how our parish life relates and is connected to the mission of Jesus. This offers an opportunity to reflect on what the mission of Jesus is for our time, in a specific locale with a specific community of God's people.

Some members on the PPC may be resistant to formulating a mission statement for the parish and might want to take a fast-track approach so that they can get on with the real work! I heard someone at a PPC workshop once say: 'Can we not just paper and paste a mission

42 Harrington, *Tomorrow's Parish*, 64.

statement from a parish in the deanery and change the name on it?' There is a certain logic to this. If we think about it, however, we can see that the process of formulating a statement has the potential to change, form and transform us. In the process of formulating the parish mission statement PPC members learn what is important to people, what makes their hearts burn, what fires them up and gets them to the church every Sunday. Formulating a parish mission statement helps the parish to become more aware of what its core purpose is and can lead to wider participation in initiatives.

PURPOSE OF A PARISH MISSION STATEMENT

The first thing that needs to be said about the purpose of a parish mission statement is that it is not meant to confirm how things were or should be. The parish mission statement is directional and aspirational. It enables the parish to have a sense that it's on a journey of development for the future. If the parish mission statement is developmental then it should provide a frame of reference or springboard for naming new actions and goals. The parish mission statement is also meant tto be unifying. It helps the parish to focus on what can be done together on the journey of faith. The parish mission statement is aspirational in that it helps to name the hopes and fears, the joys and sorrows of the lives of every day[43] but with a key focus on hope-filled outcomes. It is also inspirational in that anyone who reads it will be inspired to put something into action.

The parish mission statement needs to be of significance to a range of groups and people in the parish. It should be lengthy and in plain English. The clarity of statements it makes need to be evident to anyone who reads it. It also needs to be adaptable and changeable, many parishes take initial time to formulate a mission statement and then set it in stone for twenty years. Mission statements are not set in stone, although there will be elements in them that remain constant. If this never changes it may be a sign that the parish community is stuck and not open to a new future.

---

43   Pope Paul VI, *Gaudium et Spes*, Vatican: The Holy See, 7 December 1965, 1.

SAMPLE MISSION STATEMENTS

In order to illustrate this, here are some samples of parish mission statements. The name of the parish is invented but the statements are based on real-life parishes and how they perceive their mission.

1. Our mission is to be a warm, welcoming, inviting community where people of all ages and stages are always welcome. We are a parish with open doors and open hearts. We gather every Sunday to celebrate God's love where our energy is renewed for service and love.

2. We the parish of St Germaine's are called to be a beacon of hope and light for the world. We do this through gathering for worship, serving each other and the wider community, honouring the integrity of creation and working for a just world.

3. The mission of our parish community is to be a presence of hope and goodness in our neighbourhood. We do this by opening our doors to every person, by praying together and by proclaiming the Gospel of life, conscious that we are all called to care for God's creation.

These sample mission statements mirror the attempts of some parishes to take on a broad a range of issues that are important to parishioners. In the first statement there is a very strong emphasis on being warm and welcoming. It is only in the second sentence that the reader knows this is describing a Church community. In the final sentence of this mission statement there is a clear intention to link the celebration of liturgy with life. The second mission statement has a clear statement from the outset that it is a parish community. It aims at emphasising a 'big picture' vision of the purpose of the Church. It is more intentional than the first mission statement. Another feature of this mission statement is the emphasis on the integrity of creation, influenced by global concerns and the teachings of *Laudato Si'*. The third mission statement tries to root itself in the local community. It emphasises the importance of being an open-door community, while also honouring the importance of prayer and living a life that is rooted in the Gospel and connected to God's creation. All of these sample mission statements have a distinctive flavour. From them we can judge what each mission statement needs to include: acknowledgement that this is a Church community, the connection of the Church to the mission of Jesus, and what the Church is called to be and do.

THE PROCESS OF FORMULATING A PARISH MISSION STATEMENT

It can be very helpful when a PPC is revising its membership to take the opportunity to reflect on the parish mission statement. This could be linked to a parish assembly by intentionally inviting parishioners to explore this together. The format of the parish assembly could be about taking time to look at mission and how it is working. This parish assembly needs to be well planned in advance, and in some way inform, form and transform people. It can be informational when at the assembly various parish groups present how and what their group does in the parish. It can be formational when there is input given about a particular topic. It can be transformational when those assembled begin to see things in a new way.

The preparation for the assembly is almost as important as the event itself. Here are some easy steps and stages to follow in the preparation:

1. Decide at a PPC meeting when is the best time and place to hold the assembly. Communicate the dates and times to the parish through the parish website, Facebook page and at Masses.

2. In each week leading up to the assembly drip feed bite size pieces of information. For example, in week one inform the parish of the date and time. In week two make online

registration for the event available. In week three get individual PPC members to speak at every Mass and hand out invitations.

3. Have a series of planning meetings. Invite parishioners to be part of the planning team, offering them specific roles for the assembly. For example, who will do the greeting and welcoming? Who will make tea and coffee? Who will look after the sound system and technology? Who will set up the space? Who will be invited to facilitate? All of this and more needs to be part of the planning.

FORMAT FOR A PARISH ASSEMBLY
After this the PPC needs to agree on a format for the assembly with the facilitator. The following is only an example of what can work well.

WELCOME and INTRODUCTION/OUTLINE (5 minutes)
- The chair welcomes everyone of behalf of the PPC
- There is a power point presentation introduced with an outline of the evening
- Everyone is invited to listen well and share well

PRAYER/REFLECTION (10 – 15 minutes)
- The prayer is up on the power point for all to view and led by two members of the PPC working together
- The prayer is interactive and offers opportunity for silence too
- The prayer reminds the parish of its mission and purpose

SMALL GROUPS – First Focus (30 minutes)
- The facilitator moves on to invite small group consideration of a question
- People are put into small groups as they are gathering so that they are already in place

- The question for consideration is viewed on power point
- A possible question is 'What works well in our parish to serve the mission?'
- There is a small group leader (from the PPC), who has been trained to take feedback
- Each small group records their feedback on a Post-It note.
- This is placed on a display board for all to view

TEA and COFFEE BREAK (15 – 20 minutes)
- There is an organised tea break where parishioners are encouraged to view the responses from the small groups
- People are called back gently to their small groups after fifteen minutes

SMALL GROUPS – Second Focus (30 minutes)
- People return to their small groups
- The facilitator moves on to invite small group consideration of a second question
- The question for consideration is viewed on power point
- A possible question is 'In light of what you have heard what now needs to be developed in our parish to serve the mission?'
- There is a small group leader (from the PPC), who has been trained to take feedback
- Each small group records their feedback on a Post-It note
- This is placed on a separate display board for all to view

FACILITATOR GATHERS THE STRANDS TOGETHER (10 minutes)
- The strands of what works well are gathered together by the facilitator
- This is followed through by what needs to be developed, reminding the assembly that this is what they said

- This is handed over to the PPC to connect it to the revision of the mission statement at a later date

FINAL PRAYER MOMENT TOGETHER (10 minutes)
- The president and chair of the PPC thank all for their sharing and the meeting ends with a reflection or prayer time

BACK TO MISSION STATEMENT
After a parish assembly there is normally a lot of good energy in the parish and an expectation that things will happen. The PPC will need to meet regularly to digest what has been shared and figure out how to respond. This could take some time and be integrated into the pastoral plan. Priorities can emerge quite easily when the feedback is well collated. Feedback should be organised so that it is easy to see what people felt most strongly about. This is what is taken to prayer. It is also shared with the parish so that all are aware. As priorities emerge, the mission statement of the parish may change or the emphasis of the statement may shift. For example, where a previous mission statement emphasised the importance of gathering together as church, a revised statement might emphasise gathering together for the purpose of serving the area. A well-planned parish assembly will result not only in a revision of the mission statement but in a prioritising of a new set of pastoral activities and actions.

For Your Own Reflection

- What have you personally learned about mission in this chapter?
- How has it made you think differently about the parish?
- When have you ever thought of your life as a mission?

On Your Current PPC Practice

- What is your current parish mission statement?
- When was it last revised?
- How could you organise a parish assembly?

Useful Sources to Explore

- www.weareamission.org/popefrancis.
- Harington, *Tomorrow's Parish*, particularly chapter five.
- Pope Francis, *Laudato Si'*, Vatican: The Holy See, 24 May 2015.
- Pope Francis, *Fratelli Tutti*, Vatican: The Holy See, 3 October 2020.
- https://www.sessionlab.com/facilitation/
- Mark Fischer and Mary Margaret Raley, *Four Ways to Build More Effective Pastoral Councils*, Mystic CT: Twenty-Third Publications, 2002.
- Ron Cork, *Making Your Pastoral Council Work: A Planning Guide for Parishes*, Ottawa: Novalis, 2007.

CONCLUDING REMARKS

A PROCESS

Becoming a PPC doesn't just happen because some people have been selected to serve. It's a process that involves learning together and a journey of discovery. In this journey we discover that all of the baptised are called to participate in building up their local community, to share the life and energy that God gives us for service, and to reach out beyond the gates of the parish into the world. It comes as a surprise to many who are invited to become a PPC member that they are being invited to lead alongside the priest in a co-responsible partnership. It's an even bigger surprise to discover that in this we are responding to a call to become missionary disciples.

GROUNDED IN PRAYERFULNESS

It is also a challenge to realise that PPC members may need to grow themselves out of that passivity and procrastination that holds back the development of parish life, replacing this with a positive desire to enable everyone to fully and consciously take their part. Central to every gathering is the importance of prayer-filled consideration, without this the PPC will just remain a committee and lack the discernment to make wise decisions. When everything the PPC does is grounded, informed and guided by prayer then there is a growing sense that the Spirit is in the decisions.

In this process of becoming, the PPC can begin to notice signs of growth. Where people in the parish begin to practise collaboration, where team ministries are flourishing and community exchange is valued, these are all signs of growth to be celebrated.

ALWAYS JOURNEYING

During the writing of this book Pope Francis announced that all dioceses and parishes throughout the world are invited to embark on a synodal pathway, where listening to each other and to the voice of the Spirit becomes a permanent way of being in the Church. PPCs too can mirror this in their parish assemblies, where everyone has the opportunity to reflect on their experience in light of journeying together. It is in the parish assembly that we can begin to experience ourselves as the People of God walking together. I hope you have enjoyed your journey of discovering what a PPC is all about, and that you've realised that there is never a time when any PPC is a finished product. We are always in a process of what God is asking us to be.